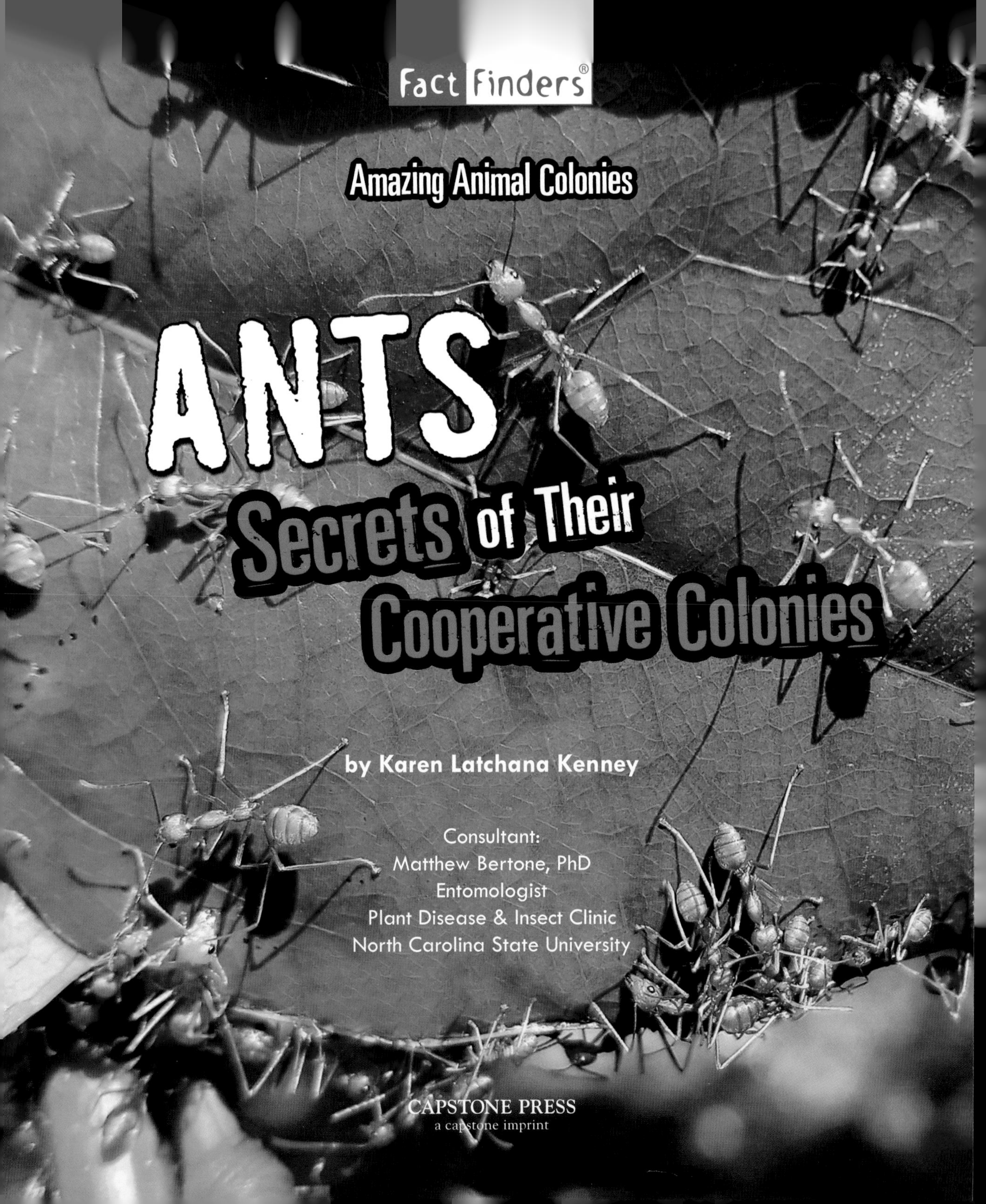

Fact Finders®

Amazing Animal Colonies

ANTS
Secrets of Their Cooperative Colonies

by Karen Latchana Kenney

Consultant:
Matthew Bertone, PhD
Entomologist
Plant Disease & Insect Clinic
North Carolina State University

CAPSTONE PRESS
a capstone imprint

Fact Finders Books are published by Capstone Press,
1710 Roe Crest Drive, North Mankato, Minnesota 56003
www.mycapstone.com

Library of Congress Cataloging-in-Publication Data
Names: Kenney, Karen Latchana, author.
Title: Ants : secrets of their cooperative colonies / by Karen Latchana
   Kenney.
Description: North Mankato, Minnesota : Capstone Press, [2019] | Series: Fact
   finders. Amazing animal colonies.
Identifiers: LCCN 2018029020 (print) | LCCN 2018035779 (ebook) | ISBN
   9781543555578 (eBook PDF) | ISBN 9781543555530 (hardcover) | ISBN
   9781543559101 (pbk.)
Subjects: LCSH: Ants—Juvenile literature. | Animal colonies—Juvenile
   literature.
Classification: LCC QL568.F7 (ebook) | LCC QL568.F7 K4395 2019 (print) | DDC
   595.79/61782—dc23
LC record available at https://lccn.loc.gov/2018029020

Editorial Credits
Editor: Carrie Braulick Sheely
Designer: Ted Williams
Media Researcher: Heather Mauldin
Production specialist: Katy LaVigne

Photo Credits
Alamy: Wachara Silitep, 11, www.pqpictures.co.uk, 18; Getty Images: John Brown, 13; iStockphoto: allgord, 15, John M. Chase, 26, pupunkkop, 29; Minden Pictures: Chien Lee, 22, Cyril Ruoso, 4, 23, Mark Moffett, 9, Paul Williams, 24-25; Science Source: Francesco Tomasinelli, 19; Shutterstock: Andrey Pavlov, cover (top), 7, Bjoern Wylezich, 6, corlaffra, 16-17, Dariusz Majgier, cover (background), Henrik Larsson, 10, ilic, 21, Ryan M. Bolton, 12, Thanisnan Sukprasert, cover (bottom), 1

Printed and bound in the USA.
PA48

Table of Contents

Chapter One
STRENGTH IN NUMBERS 4

Chapter Two
THE LIVES OF ANTS 8

Chapter Three
ANT COMMUNICATION AND BEHAVIOR 14

Chapter Four
BUILDING BIG NESTS 20

Chapter Five
ANTS AND PEOPLE............................ 26

Glossary............................. 30
Read More 31
Critical Thinking Questions 31
Internet Sites............................ 31
Index 32

CHAPTER ONE
STRENGTH IN NUMBERS

Soldier driver ants stand on the edges of a column to guard the worker ants.

An inky black mass spreads across the ground. It moves like liquid, snaking forward little by little. Soon it covers more than 200 feet (60 meters). The mass is made of millions of driver ants. They move in lines called columns. Large soldier ants stand guard at the sides of each column. Smaller worker ants run in the middle of the columns. As the worker ants move, they kill anything in their path. They cut up scorpions, snakes, termites, and other creatures they find. Then they bring the food back to their nest. This army of ants works as a team. Together they are a powerful force.

On its own, an ant may not be very strong or smart. But all ants work in groups called **colonies**. Each ant cooperates with the other ants in the colony. The colony is very organized. Every ant has certain jobs it performs. Worker ants go out to find food. They also take care of the young. Soldier ants defend the nest. The division of work helps make sure the colony survives. Scientists call a colony that ants form a **superorganism**. The colony may have millions of members, but it acts as a whole.

colony—a large group of insects that live together
superorganism—a group of living things that work together as a whole

Insect Survivors

Ants are one of the most successful creatures on Earth. They've been around for more than 100 million years. At that time, dinosaurs roamed Earth.

Many of the oldest ant **fossils** were trapped in **amber** from ancient trees. In 1998 scientists found some of the oldest ant fossils in amber in New Jersey.

Today more than 13,000 ant **species** exist. Ants live almost everywhere. The only places where they don't live are very cold places, including the Arctic and Antarctica. There are also a few islands with no ants.

an ant fossil
preserved in amber

6

All ants are insects. They have three main body parts. These are a head, thorax, and abdomen. Ants have six legs. Two antennae help them smell what's around them. Their main tools are jaws called mandibles. Ants use them to grip, cut, build, and fight. Ants range in size from 0.08 inch (2 millimeters) to 1 inch (25 mm) long.

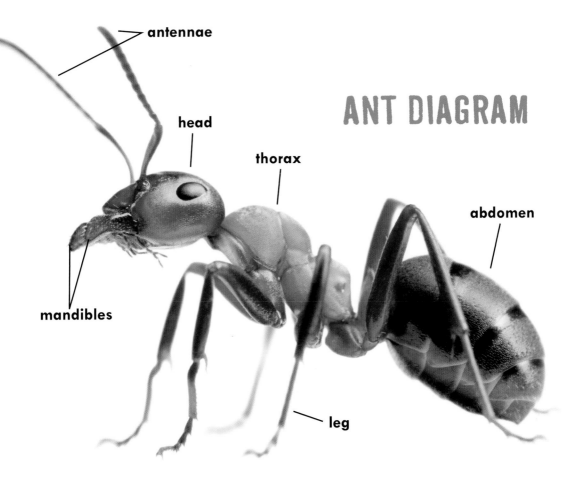

ANT DIAGRAM

antennae

head

thorax

abdomen

mandibles

leg

fossil—the remains or traces of plants and animals that are preserved as rock
amber—a yellowish-brown substance formed from fossilized tree sap
species—a group of closely related organisms that can produce offspring

CHAPTER TWO

THE LIVES OF ANTS

The number of ants in a colony varies according to species. Some ant colonies are very small. One lives in the Amazon Rain Forest in South America. Its colonies have only four members. Other ant colonies are huge. Army and driver ant colonies have millions of members. The Argentine ant even has supercolonies. In these colonies two or more individual colonies join. In the early 2000s, one of the Argentine ant's supercolonies spanned more than 3,700 miles (5,950 kilometers) in southern Europe. It contained billions of workers. It was the largest supercolony ever recorded.

AMAZING FACT

Of the about 13,000 ant species, only about 20 are known to form supercolonies.

A New Colony Begins

Each ant colony begins with a queen. A queen is the only ant that can produce young in the colony. After she grows to an adult, a queen uses her wings to fly away from her original home. She mates with winged male ants called drones. The drones die soon after mating. The queen then finds a good place to make her nest.

Argentine ants feed on the tip of a shrub. They eat both plants and animals.

↑ant larvae

From Egg to Adult

After finding a new home, the queen sheds her wings. Soon she lays her first eggs. The eggs look like small grains of white rice. She cares for the first eggs. The eggs develop into **larvae** that look like clear worms. Then the larvae go through a big change into **pupae**. Some change inside a **cocoon**. The pupae look like clear ants. As they grow, they darken in color. Finally, they become adults.

larva—an insect at the stage of development between an egg and a pupa when it looks like a worm

pupa—an insect at the stage of development between a larva and an adult

cocoon—a covering made of silky thread; insects make a cocoon to protect themselves while they change from larvae to pupae

The queen's first eggs become workers as adults. All workers are female, but they can't reproduce. As the queen lays more eggs, the workers start caring for the young.

ANT LIFE CYCLE

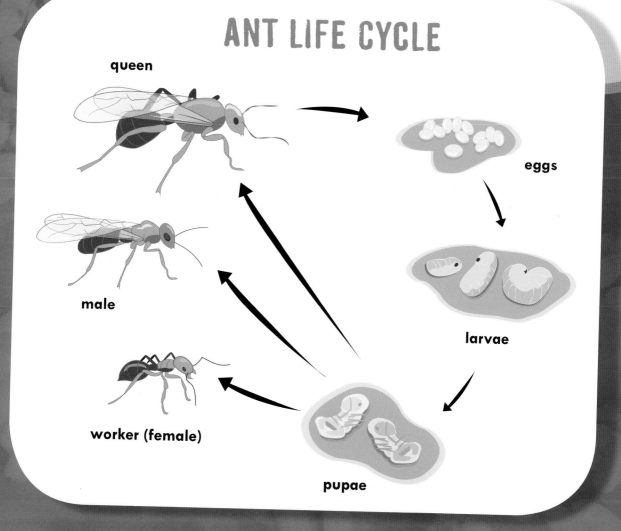

queen

eggs

male

larvae

worker (female)

pupae

A Job for All

The workers are one type of caste. Other castes are queens, drones, and soldiers. Each caste does a certain job in the colony. How does an ant get its job? Chemical signals tell workers what castes are needed. The workers feed the larvae different amounts of food. This changes what kind of adult the ant will become. Most larvae become workers. Some kinds of ants have several sizes of workers. Very few larvae become new queens and drones.

Workers are very busy. They care for the larvae and the queen. They build and fix the nest and remove the ants' waste. They find food, such as insects or seeds. The workers bring the food back to the nest.

Some ant species have a soldier caste. Soldiers are much larger than the workers. They have big heads and powerful jaws. They protect the colony from enemies.

Worker leafcutter ants carry leaves back to their colony.

LIVING REFRIGERATORS: HONEYPOT ANTS

Honeypot ants live in dry, desert areas. Their food is flower nectar. During rainy seasons, there is plenty of nectar. But in dry seasons, nectar can be hard to find. Special worker ants are in some rooms of a honeypot ant nest. They cling to the ceiling and let their bodies hang down. They cannot walk on the ground. That's because their abdomens are the size of grapes. Inside them is stored nectar. It's food for the colony. When ants in the colony are hungry, the food-storing ants spit up some nectar. They help the colony survive.

13

CHAPTER THREE

ANT COMMUNICATION AND BEHAVIOR

Ants work together like the parts of a machine. But how do they know when to do each task? Their communication is the key to making the colony run smoothly.

Ants can't talk, and they can't see very well. There isn't one leader of an ant colony either. So how do ants communicate? One main way is by sensing chemicals. These chemicals are called pheromones. Ants also vibrate their bodies and use touch to communicate.

Ants have developed a whole set of pheromones they use to communicate. Each one says something different. When they are mixed, they say something else. Some chemicals say, "Follow me!" Others say, "This way to the nest." Others say, "Danger!"

Some chemicals last much longer on the ground. A chemical used to get more ants to follow may last just a few minutes. But a chemical to say where food is lasts longer.

Ants often form long trails as they sense chemicals on the ground.

AMAZING FACT

Sometimes ants shake their bodies. The shaking makes their chemicals have a stronger scent. This helps them get more ants to go where they are needed.

Scientists have found 12 different types of ant communication. They include signals for alarm, food location, to gather, and to make a certain caste. Chemicals also help ants tell one another apart. Ants from the same colony have a similar smell. But the smell of the workers and queen ants are not exactly the same. Scientists believe the different smells help ants know the roles of one another.

Several ants follow chemical trails from the nest to food sources. They may need to work together to carry large amounts of food back to the nest.

Follow the Leader

Some ant species get other ants to follow them using mainly touch. When an ant finds food, it lays down chemicals. But only it knows what the chemicals mean. It finds a nestmate willing to follow it. It turns around and starts running. The other ant touches the first ant's back legs with its antennae. It runs right behind the first ant. This is called tandem running. The process continues until both reach the food source. Sometimes the follower later becomes a leader for another ant.

Danger!

Ant **predators** include anteaters, spiders, and other ants. One chemical signal tells other ants that danger is near. Then the soldiers kick into action. Many ants sting predators or attack with their strong jaws. Some soldiers can make their poison-filled bodies explode. The individual ants die after exploding, but their sacrifice helps the colony.

Some soldiers can spray chemicals. Wood ants make a kind of acid in their bodies. They curl up their abdomens. Then they spray the acid into the air. When one ant smells the acid, it starts spraying too. Soon hundreds of ants are spraying acid. The acid is strong enough to scare away predators as large as birds.

Wood ants spray chemicals to defend their nest.

Fire ants quickly defend their nests.

FIRE ANTS

Fire ants are known for being aggressive defenders. If their nest is disturbed, thousands of them stream out. They start stinging the attacker. If a person steps on a fire ant nest, the ants often run up the person's legs and arms. As each ant stings, it injects **venom** with its stinger. The stings cause painful itchy bumps. Some people are allergic to fire ant venom. If they are stung, they need to be treated in a hospital. Without treatment, they can die.

predator—an animal that hunts other animals for food

venom—a poisonous liquid produced by some animals

CHAPTER FOUR

BUILDING BIG NESTS

Ant colonies live in nests. They build them in many different places in different ways.

Underground Nests

Most ants build nests underground. Their entrances look like tiny volcanoes of dirt or sand. They go into the nest through a hole in the middle. It leads to long tunnels. Rooms called chambers branch off from these tunnels. The chambers have different uses. Some hold the eggs, larvae, and pupae. Some store food. Some hold waste. One may hold the queen.

Worker ants continually fix and build their underground nests. They push dirt and sticks out of the way with their heads. They grab small rocks and dirt with their jaws. They bring the dirt through the hole that sticks up through the entrance. Then they drop it off outside. This makes the anthills you see on top of the ground.

Ants often leave mounds of dirt at their nest entrances.

Scouting a New Nest

Sometimes a colony needs to move. It may get too big for its nest. Its nest might start caving in. Or maybe another colony has moved in too close. The other ants compete for food in the area. If this happens, workers called scouts go out to search for a new nest site.

A nest has to be the right size and shape for the whole colony. When a scout finds a good site, it returns to the old nest. It releases chemicals to get other ants to follow it. If those ants agree that the site is good, they return to the old nest. They get even more ants to follow. Then the whole colony moves. Workers carry the young ants and ant eggs. They carry some adults too.

LIVING NESTS

Some ant species never build a lasting nest. They are always on the move. Instead, they build short-lived nests with their bodies. These nests are called bivouacs. Many army ants make bivouacs each night after a raid. The queen, larvae, and pupae are at its center. Workers huddle together all around them. They grip one another's legs to form the nest's living walls. Soldiers gather on the top, ready to defend the nest. The next morning, the nest breaks apart. Then the ants go on their next raid.

Extreme Nests

Some ants have very unique nests. You might even call some of them extreme! Some ants build large mounds above ground. Others build nests in trees or sticks. Tiny yellow acorn ants make their nests inside acorns.

Harvester ant workers build huge underground cities. They reach skyscraper-like heights for the ant's small size. Their nests have layers of flat chambers that all connect.

an Allegheny mound ant nest

Mound ants are some of the strongest builders. The Allegheny mound ant can lift objects 5,000 times its own weight! Workers build a mound from sand, twigs, and leaves. The mound can be 3 feet (0.9 m) tall and 6 feet (1.8 m) wide.

Leafcutter ants make complex underground nests. These ants grow their food in underground gardens. The gardens are in certain chambers of their nest. Worker ants find and cut leaves to add to their gardens. The leaves feed a fungus in the gardens. The ants eat the fungus. Worker ants take

care of the gardens. They put the waste in other chambers. A nest that's six years old can have close to 2,000 chambers. The soil the ants remove to make it can weigh 6 tons.

AMAZING FACT

Weaver ants build nests high in trees using leaves. To start, some workers act like staples, stretching their bodies to hold leaves together. Later other workers glue the leaves together with silk.

CHAPTER FIVE

ANTS AND PEOPLE

Carpenter ants can cause damage to buildings quickly. Signs of an infestation include rectangular openings in the wood.

Ants live almost everywhere. They are some of the world's most plentiful insects. People come into contact with them often. Ants help people in many ways. They can be problems in other ways.

Invading Ants

Ants often invade people's homes. They find their way into walls, kitchens, and more. They search for crumbs of food to eat and places to build their nests. They become pests that people can have a hard time removing from their homes.

Some ants can even damage buildings. Carpenter ants often build their nests inside rotting wood. They dig long tunnels in the wood. This wood could be inside a dead tree. But sometimes they build nests in the walls of homes. If a nest gets big enough, it can make walls weak. The wood breaks apart and the walls could fall down.

Snacking on Ants

Some people want to find ants for their next snack! Many native Australians called Aborigines search for honeypot ants. When they find them, they hold them by their heads. Then they bite off their sweet abdomens as treats. In Colombia some people search for new queen leafcutter ants in spring. People roast the ants and salt them. They eat them like peanuts. In Southeast Asia, people use ant eggs in a soup. The eggs pop when they are eaten.

Cleaning Up and Helping Plants Grow

Ants help the environment. They are called **detritivores** because they break down waste in nature. They eat dead creatures. They dig inside dead trees. The trees then rot faster.

Ants that live underground help the soil. As they dig, they leave spaces in the soil. The spaces help water trickle down into the dirt to help crops grow. Underground ants also help plants grow by keeping the soil light and airy.

detritivore—an organism that feeds on dead and rotting material in nature

Some ants hunt other animals. These ants can help control pests on crops. People have used weaver ants to help control pests in fruit orchards and cashew trees.

We share our world with many kinds of ants. They're incredible survivors. Although they can cause problems, they have important roles. The next time you see one, remember what this small creature does to help us!

Ants feed on a dead grasshopper.

Index

Amazon Rain Forest, 8
Argentine ants, 8

bivouacs, 23

carpenter ants, 27
castes, 12, 16
chemicals, 12, 14, 15, 16, 17, 18, 22

driver ants, 5, 8
drones, 9, 12

eggs, 10, 11, 20, 22, 28

fire ants, 19
fossils, 6

harvester ants, 24
honeypot ants, 13, 28

insects, 7, 12, 27

larvae, 10, 12, 20, 22, 23
leafcutter ants, 25, 28

mound ants, 25

nests, 5, 9, 12, 13, 14, 19, 20, 22, 23, 24, 25, 27

pheromones, 14
pupae, 10, 11, 20, 23

queens, 9, 10, 11, 12, 16, 20, 23, 28

supercolonies, 8

tandem running, 17

weaver ants, 25, 29